Abraham Lincoln.

Abraham Lincoln.

An Horatian Ode.

By Richard Henry Stoddard.

NEW YORK:
BUNCE & HUNTINGTON, PUBLISHERS,
540 BROADWAY.

ALVORD, PRINTER.

Abraham Lincoln:

Born, Feb. 12th, 1809,

Assassinated, Good-Friday, April 14th, 1865.

"Confusion now hath made his masterpiece!
Most sacrilegious murder hath broke ope
The Lord's anointed temple, and stole thence
The life o' the building.
* * * * * * *
"Approach the chamber, and destroy your sight
With a new Gorgon:—Do not bid me speak;
See, and then speak yourselves.—Awake! awake!
Ring the alarum-bell:—Murder! and treason!
* * * * * * *
"Shake off this downy sleep, death's counterfeit,
And look on death itself!—up, up, and see
The great doom's image!
* * * * * * *
"Our royal master's murdered!
* * * * * * *
"Had I but died an hour before this chance,
I had lived a blessed time; for from this instant
There's nothing serious in mortality:
All is but toys: renown and grace is dead;
The wine of life is drawn, and the mere lees
Is left this vault to brag of.

"After life's fitful fever, he sleeps well;
Treason has done his worst: nor steel, nor poison,
Malice domestic, foreign levy, nothing,
Can touch him further."

Macbeth.

NOT as when some great Captain falls
In battle, where his Country calls,
Beyond the struggling lines
That push his dread designs

To doom, by some stray ball struck dead:
Or, in the last charge, at the head
Of his determined men,
Who *must* be victors then!

Nor as when sink the civic Great,
The safer pillars of the State,
Whose calm, mature, wise words
Suppress the need of swords!—

With no such tears as e'er were shed
Above the noblest of our Dead
Do we to-day deplore
The Man that is no more!

Our sorrow hath a wider scope,
Too strange for fear, too vast for hope,—
        A Wonder, blind and dumb,
        That waits—what is to come!

Not more astounded had we been
If Madness, that dark night, unseen,
        Had in our chambers crept,
        And murdered while we slept!

We woke to find a mourning Earth—
Our Lares shivered on the hearth,—
        The roof-tree fallen,—all
        That could affright, appall!

Such thunderbolts, in other lands,
Have smitten the rod from royal hands,
        But spared, with us, till now,
        Each laurelled Cesar's brow!

No Cesar he, whom we lament,
A Man without a precedent,
        Sent, it would seem, to do
        His work—and perish too!

Not by the weary cares of State,
The endless tasks, which will not wait,
        Which, often done in vain,
        Must yet be done again:

Not in the dark, wild tide of War,
Which rose so high, and rolled so far,
        Sweeping from sea to sea
        In awful anarchy:—

Four fateful years of mortal strife,
Which slowly drained the Nation's life,
(Yet, for each drop that ran
There sprang an armed man!)

Not then;—but when by measures meet,—
By victory, and by defeat,—
By courage, patience, skill,
The People's fixed "*We will!*"

Had pierced, had crushed Rebellion dead,—
Without a Hand, without a Head:—
At last, when all was well,
He fell—O, *how* he fell!

The time,—the place,—the stealing Shape,—
The coward shot,—the swift escape,—
The wife—the widow's scream,—
It is a hideous Dream!

A Dream?—what means this pageant, then?
These multitudes of solemn men,
Who speak not when they meet,
But throng the silent street?

The flags half-mast, that late so high
Flaunted at each new victory?
(The stars no brightness shed,
But bloody looks the red!)

The black festoons that stretch for miles,
And turn the streets to funeral aisles?
(No house too poor to show
The Nation's badge of woe!)

The cannon's sudden, sullen boom,—
The bells that toll of death and doom,—
　　The rolling of the drums,—
　　The dreadful Car that comes?

Cursed be the hand that fired the shot!
The frenzied brain that hatched the plot!
　　Thy Country's Father slain
　　By thee, thou worse than Cain!

Tyrants have fallen by such as thou,
And Good hath followed—May it now!
　　(God lets bad instruments
　　Produce the best events.)

But he, the Man we mourn to-day,
No tyrant was: so mild a sway
　　In one such weight who bore
　　Was never known before!

Cool should he be, of balanced powers,
The Ruler of a Race like ours,
　　Impatient, headstrong, wild,—
　　The Man to guide the Child!

And this *he* was, who most unfit
(So hard the sense of God to hit!)
　　Did seem to fill his Place.
　　With such a homely face,—

Such rustic manners,—speech uncouth,—
(That somehow blundered out the Truth!)
　　Untried, untrained to bear
　　The more than kingly Care?

Ay! And his genius put to scorn
The proudest in the purple born,
Whose wisdom never grew
To what, untaught, he knew—

The People, of whom he was one.
No gentleman like Washington,—
(Whose bones, methinks, make room,
To have him in their tomb!)

A laboring man, with horny hands,
Who swung the axe, who tilled his lands,
Who shrank from nothing new,
But did as poor men do!

One of the People! Born to be
Their curious Epitome;
To share, yet rise above
Their shifting hate and love.

Common his mind (it seemed so then),
His thoughts the thoughts of other men:
Plain were his words, and poor—
But now they will endure!

No hasty fool, of stubborn will,
But prudent, cautious, pliant, still;
Who, since his work was good,
Would do it, as he could.

Doubting, was not ashamed to doubt,
And, lacking prescience, went without:
Often appeared to halt,
And was, of course, at fault:

Heard all opinions, nothing loth,
And loving both sides, angered both:
Was—*not* like Justice, blind,
But watchful, clement, kind.

No hero, this, of Roman mould;
Nor like our stately sires of old:
Perhaps he was not Great—
But he preserved the State!

O honest face, which all men knew!
O tender heart, but known to few!
O Wonder of the Age,
Cut off by tragic Rage!

Peace! Let the long procession come,
For hark!—the mournful, muffled drum—
The trumpet's wail afar,—
And see! the awful Car!

Peace! Let the sad procession go,
While cannon boom, and bells toll slow:
And go, thou sacred Car,
Bearing our Woe afar!

Go, darkly borne, from State to State,
Whose loyal, sorrowing Cities wait
To honor all they can
The dust of that Good Man!

Go, grandly borne, with such a train
As greatest kings might die to gain:
The Just, the Wise, the Brave
Attend thee to the grave!

And you, the soldiers of our wars,
Bronzed veterans, grim with noble scars,
Salute him once again,
Your late Commander—slain!

Yes, let your tears, indignant, fall,
But leave your muskets on the wall:
Your Country needs you now
Beside the forge, the plough!

(When Justice shall unsheathe her brand,—
If Mercy may not stay her hand,
Nor would we have it so—
She must direct the blow!)

And you, amid the Master-Race,
Who seem so strangely out of place,
Know ye who cometh? He
Who hath declared ye Free!

Bow while the Body passes—Nay,
Fall on your knees, and weep, and pray!
Weep, weep—I would ye might—
Your poor, black faces white!

And, Children, you must come in bands,
With garlands in your little hands,
Of blue, and white, and red,
To strew before the Dead!

So, sweetly, sadly, sternly goes
The Fallen to his last repose:
Beneath no mighty dome,
But in his modest Home;

The churchyard where his children rest,
The quiet spot that suits him best:
    There shall his grave be made,
    And there his bones be laid!

And there his countrymen shall come,
With memory proud, with pity dumb,
    And strangers far and near,
    For many and many a year!

For many a year, and many an Age,
While History on her ample page
    The virtues shall enroll
    Of that Paternal Soul!

www.ingramcontent.com/pod-product-compliance
Lightning Source LLC
LaVergne TN
LVHW020638110826
845149LV00004B/1268

* 9 7 8 1 4 1 8 1 8 9 6 8 6 *